How to Delete Books from Kindle Devices

Step by Step Guide to Delete Books from Your Kindle in Minutes (Delete from Kindle, Delete from Library, Delete on All Devices)

Corey Stone

including specific information will be considered an illegal act irrespective of if it is done electronically or in print. This extends to creating a secondary or tertiary copy of the work or a recorded copy and is only allowed with express written consent from the Publisher. All additional rights reserved.

The information in the following pages is broadly considered to be a truthful and accurate account of facts and as such any inattention, use or misuse of the information in question by the reader will render any resulting actions solely under their purview. There are no scenarios in which the publisher or the original author of this work can be in any fashion deemed liable for any hardship or damages that may befall them after undertaking information described herein.

Additionally, the information in the following pages is intended only for informational purposes and should thus be thought of as universal. As befitting its nature, it is presented without assurance regarding its prolonged validity or interim quality. Trademarks that are mentioned are done without written consent and can in no way be considered an endorsement from the trademark holder.

TABLE OF CONTENTS

Introduction

Congratulations on downloading *How to Delete Books from Kindle Devices* and thank you for doing so.

The following chapters will discuss each step that you will need to know so that you can remove a book from any Kindle device that you own. This will include the applications that you will use with Kindle.

There are plenty of books on this subject on the market, thanks again for choosing this one! Every effort was made to ensure it is full of as much useful information as possible, please enjoy!

Chapter One: The Difference Between Removing Books

Your Kindle has three different areas where your books will be located: the cloud, your device, your library. Sometimes, there are books that you are no longer going to want to have on your account, and you will need to delete them. But, you cannot delete the book from one section of your Amazon account and expect it to be removed from every other area of your account.

Removing a book from the cloud means that you will be getting rid of the book for good. This is typically going to be done when you do not want the book anymore because you did not like it, or you accidentally bought it, and you cannot get a refund for it (since some Kindle books are not eligible for a refund).

When you remove a book from your library, you will still be able to download it back to your Kindle when you want it because it will be in your cloud. Removing it from the library will make room in your library if you need some more room for new books.

Removing a book from your device will keep it in your library, but it will no longer be available on the device you use when you are reading your Kindle books.

Chapter Two: Removing Books from Your Kindle Devices

Removing items from the content library

1. Navigate to the page entitled "manage your content and devices."

2. From the content tab, you will change the show menu to the category you need to see.

3. Choose the book you want to delete and push the delete button.

4. Confirm that you want to delete the item permanently.

Removing items from Kindle cloud/content cloud

1. Log into your account

2. Click on your account

3. Move to manage content and devices

4. Locate your book

5. Left click on the title and select delete

Removing books from your Kindle device

1. Go to your Kindle library

2. Find the title that you want to get rid of

3. Press and hold the title to remove it. There will be a menu that pops up where you will be able to choose the delete option.

Delete a book from Kindle Fire

1. Press and hold onto the book title.

2. Select the remove from device option out of the three options that you see.

3. Confirm your choice.

Delete a book from Kindle Fire HD

1. On the home screen, go to books so that your library is displayed.

2. Find the title you want to delete.

3. Press and hold the item that you want to remove.

4. A menu will appear, and you will choose the remove from device option.

Deleting a book from Kindle Keyboard

1. Go to your book library

2. Use the left toggle on your five-way controller

3. Move the option down to the remove from device option

4. Press your five-way controller

Delete a book from Kindle app for iOS

1. Open your Kindle application.

2. Move to your library.

3. Make sure you can see all the books in your library.

4. Locate the book you want to get rid of and swipe left to delete the book.

5. In grid mode, press and hold to get the menu that will allow you to delete the book.

Deleting a book from Kindle app for Android

1. Go to the Kindle library.

2. Press and hold on the title you want to delete.

3. A checkmark will appear. This will let you pick several books at once.

4. Press the trash can that appears at the top.

Chapter Three: Alternative Ways to Delete Books

Archiving books on your Kindle

1. Turn on your Kindle

2. Use the 5-way controller to get to your library

3. Push right on the 5-way controller

4. Move down to remove from device option

5. Press the center button to select this option.

When you archive a book, you will be moving the book to your Amazon cloud so that you can access it later. You will need to follow the steps outlined above to delete it from the cloud if you no longer want it on your Amazon account.

Deregistering your Kindle device

1. Go to the *"manage your content and devices"* tab on a computer.

2. Navigate to the tab labeled "your devices."

3. Select the device that you want to deregister.

4. Click on deregister.

1. If you want to use your Kindle after you have deregistered it, you will need to re-register it so that it can be added back to your Amazon account. If you do not want it on your account, you always have the option of adding it to a different Amazon account. Regardless of

the account that is being used, it will need to be registered so that all of Amazon's features can be used.

Conclusion

Thank you for making it through to the end of *How to Delete Books from Kindle Devices*, let's hope it was informative and able to provide you with all of the tools you need to achieve your goals whatever it may be.

The next step is to delete any book on your Kindle devices that you no longer want. You may not have a book to delete by now, but you will at some point in time. And thanks to this book. It has helped you know how to delete a book whether it is from your device, library, or cloud.

Finally, if you found this book useful in any way,

a review on Amazon is always appreciated!

Thank you and good luck!

Check Out Other Books

Please go here to check out other books that might interest you:

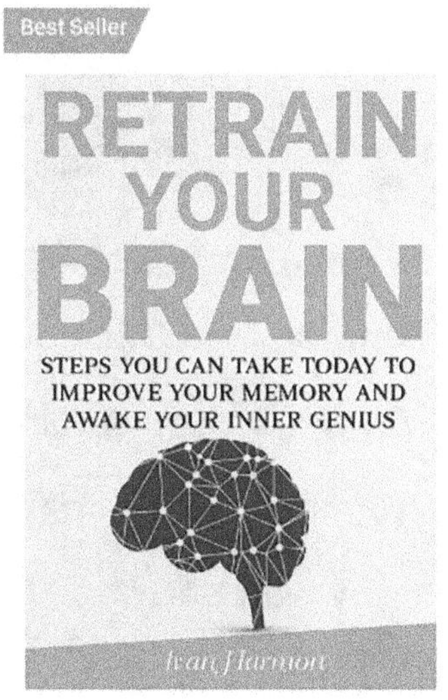

Retrain Your Brain: Steps You Can Take Today to Improve Your Memory and Awake Your Inner Genius by Ivan Harmon

Enhance Memory: Find Out How Memory Functions, Switch On Your Brain and Have Better Memory - two-book bundle

by Ivan Harmon

Boost Your Brain Power: Learn Better, Smarter, and faster - Scientifically Proven Guides to Sharpen Your Focus and Retrain Your Brain

by Ivan Harmon

10 Fun Facts About Your Memory

by Ivan Harmon

10 Interesting Facts About Your Own Mind that You Probably Don't Know

by Ivan Harmon

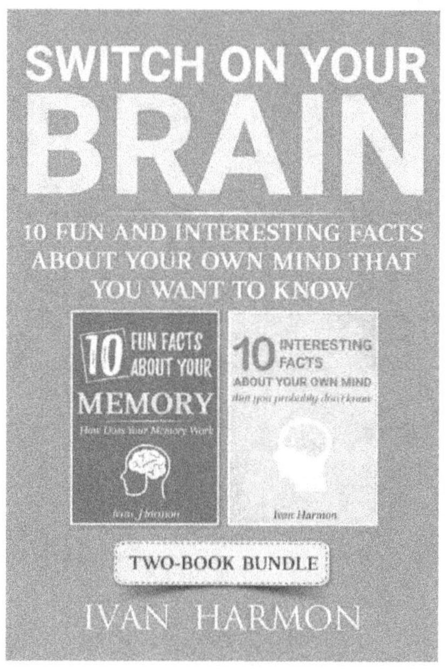

Switch On Your Brain: 10 Fun and Interesting Facts About Your Own Mind that You Want to Know by Ivan Harmon

Memory Exercises: Create a habit for memory enhancement by Ivan Harmon

Have Better Memory: Your Memory How It Works and How to Improve It by Ivan Harmon

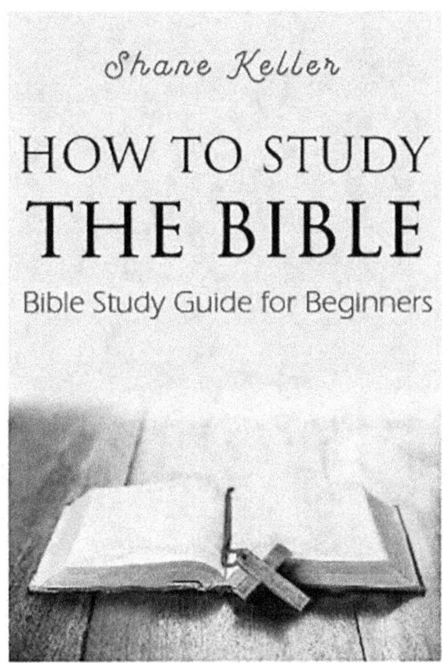

How to Study the Bible: Bible Study Guide for Beginners by Shane Keller

Know your Bible: How to Memorize the Bible

Fast and Easy

by Shane Keller

Bible Study Guide for Beginners: How to Memorize the Bible Fast and Easy

by Shane Keller

Mastering Bitcoin for Starters: Bitcoin Investment Basics - Tips for Success

by Leon Watson

What Your Boss Never Wants You to Know:

How to Find Your Strengths, Work Happier,

Grow Your Expertise, and Rediscover Your Life

by Lam Thanh Hue

www.ingramcontent.com/pod-product-compliance
Lightning Source LLC
Chambersburg PA
CBHW060823260726
48660CB00003B/1069